The Instant Focus Formula

The Instant Focus Formula

Matthew Petchinsky

The Instant Focus Formula: Cut Through the Noise
By: Matthew Petchinsky

Introduction: Mastering Focus in a Distracted World

In today's fast-paced world, the ability to focus has become both a rare and precious skill. From the moment we wake up, we are bombarded with notifications, advertisements, and endless streams of information vying for our attention. Smartphones chime with updates, social media platforms encourage mindless scrolling, and multitasking is often glorified as the hallmark of productivity. Yet, amidst this noise, many of us feel a growing sense of frustration, disconnection, and overwhelm. Why? Because the constant distractions pull us away from our goals, our creativity, and even our sense of self.

Staying focused in a world of perpetual distractions is no small feat. Our brains are wired to seek novelty, making it all too easy to succumb to the lure of a buzzing phone or an intriguing headline. Add to this the societal pressures to stay connected and always available, and it's no wonder so many people struggle to concentrate. The consequences are profound: tasks take longer to complete, creativity suffers, and mental exhaustion becomes a constant companion. In extreme cases, this lack of focus can even erode our sense of purpose, leaving us feeling unproductive and unfulfilled.

But what if there was a way to take back control? What if you could cut through the noise, refocus your mind, and channel your energy into what truly matters? This is where the **Instant Focus Formula** comes in—a simple yet powerful method for regaining mental clarity and maintaining it in any environment.

The Instant Focus Formula is not just a productivity hack or a fleeting trend; it's a practical, repeatable approach designed to help you master your attention. By implementing this formula, you'll learn how to shield your mind from distractions, cultivate laser-like focus, and reclaim the time and energy that distractions often steal. Whether you're working on a critical project, pursuing a creative passion, or simply trying to enjoy a moment of peace, this method will serve as your anchor in the storm of distractions.

The Benefits of Mastering Focus

Mastering focus is about far more than just getting things done. It's about unlocking your full potential in every aspect of life. When you have control over your attention, you'll experience:

1. **Heightened Productivity:** Focus allows you to work smarter, not harder. With clear attention, you'll accomplish tasks more efficiently and with greater precision, freeing up time for other pursuits.

2. **Enhanced Creativity:** When distractions are minimized, your mind has the space to think deeply, explore new ideas, and connect seemingly unrelated concepts. This is the foundation of true innovation.

3. **Improved Well-Being:** The ability to focus reduces stress and mental fatigue, creating a sense of calm and control. It also fosters deeper connections with others, as you become fully present in conversations and relationships.

4. **Stronger Resilience:** In a world of constant interruptions, the ability to focus acts as a shield against overwhelm. It empowers you to navigate challenges with clarity and determination.

5. **Greater Sense of Fulfillment:** When you can direct your attention toward meaningful goals, you'll find greater satisfaction in your achievements and in life itself.

This book is your guide to mastering focus in an age of distractions. Through practical strategies, actionable insights, and the Instant Focus Formula, you'll learn how to transform your mind into a powerful tool for achieving your dreams. Whether you're a busy professional, a student, or someone seeking balance in a chaotic world, the principles outlined here will empower you to harness the power of attention and thrive in all areas of life.

Now, let's dive into the Instant Focus Formula and begin the journey to a more focused, productive, and fulfilling life.

Chapter 1: The Psychology of Focus

In a world teeming with distractions, understanding the psychology of focus is the first step toward mastering it. Focus is not merely about willpower; it is deeply rooted in the intricate workings of our brain. By exploring the science behind attention and identifying common barriers, we can begin to unlock the tools needed to regain control of our mental faculties.

The Science Behind Attention

At its core, focus is the brain's ability to concentrate on specific information while filtering out irrelevant stimuli. This process, known as **selective attention**, is governed by several interconnected brain regions, most notably the **prefrontal cortex** and the **anterior cingulate cortex**.

- **The Prefrontal Cortex**: This area, located at the front of the brain, is responsible for executive functions such as decision-making, planning, and maintaining attention. It acts as the brain's "command center," directing focus and prioritizing tasks.
- **The Anterior Cingulate Cortex**: This region works alongside the prefrontal cortex to monitor distractions and resolve conflicts between competing stimuli. For example, it helps you stay on task when you're tempted to check your phone during a meeting.

The brain's attentional system operates in two modes:

1. **Top-Down Processing**: This is a deliberate, goal-oriented form of focus where you consciously direct your attention. For instance, reading a book or solving a problem requires top-down attention.
2. **Bottom-Up Processing**: This is an automatic response to external stimuli, such as the sudden sound of a phone notification or a

bright billboard. Bottom-up attention is instinctive and often interrupts our top-down focus.

Modern life heavily taxes both modes of attention, often overloading the brain with stimuli. To maintain focus, we must learn to manage these attentional processes effectively.

Common Barriers to Focus

Several factors make it increasingly difficult to sustain attention in today's world. By recognizing these barriers, you can begin to address and mitigate their effects.

1. Multitasking

Contrary to popular belief, the brain is not designed to multitask. When we try to juggle multiple tasks at once, we're not actually doing them simultaneously. Instead, the brain rapidly switches between tasks, a phenomenon known as **task-switching**. This constant shifting depletes cognitive resources, leading to:

- Decreased efficiency.
- Increased error rates.
- Mental fatigue.

2. Digital Overload

The sheer volume of digital information we consume daily overwhelms the brain's attentional system. Endless notifications, emails, and social media updates create a cycle of distraction that:

- Shortens attention spans.
- Reduces the brain's ability to prioritize important tasks.
- Reinforces habits of constant checking and scrolling.

3. Decision Fatigue

Every decision we make, no matter how small, drains mental energy. From choosing what to wear to deciding what to eat, these tiny choices accumulate throughout the day. By the time we reach the afternoon, our ability to concentrate wanes, and we're more susceptible to distractions.

A Simple Exercise to Assess Focus Levels

Before embarking on the journey to improved focus, it's essential to understand your current level of concentration. The following exercise will help you evaluate your attention span and identify areas for improvement.

Focus Assessment Exercise

1. **Set a Timer**: Find a quiet space and set a timer for 10 minutes.
2. **Choose a Task**: Select a simple activity that requires sustained attention, such as reading a paragraph from a book or solving a puzzle.
3. **Track Your Distractions**: As you work on the task, use a piece of paper to tally every time your mind wanders or you feel the urge to check your phone, look away, or think about something unrelated.
4. **Evaluate Your Results**:
   - **0–2 distractions**: Strong focus and concentration.
   - **3–5 distractions**: Moderate focus; room for improvement.
   - **6+ distractions**: High level of distractibility; consider strategies to strengthen focus.

Repeat this exercise under different conditions (e.g., in a quiet room versus a noisy environment) to identify how external factors influence your attention.

Conclusion

Understanding the psychology of focus reveals that attention is a finite resource shaped by both internal brain mechanisms and external influences. By recognizing the impact of multitasking, digital overload, and decision fatigue, you can begin to take steps toward regaining control. The assessment exercise provides a starting point to evaluate your focus and track your progress as you implement the strategies in the following chapters.

Focus is a skill that can be developed, and with the right tools and knowledge, you can transform your ability to concentrate and thrive in any environment. Let's dive deeper into the Instant Focus Formula in the next chapter to build upon this foundation.

Chapter 2: Building Your Focus Toolkit

Focus is a skill, and like any skill, it requires the right tools and techniques to cultivate. In this chapter, we will explore a variety of proven methods to enhance your ability to concentrate. From time management strategies like time-blocking and the Pomodoro Technique to mindfulness practices and creating a distraction-free environment, you'll discover practical ways to build a toolkit that empowers you to stay focused in any situation.

Key Techniques for Improving Focus

1. Time-Blocking

Time-blocking is a simple yet powerful time management strategy that involves dividing your day into blocks dedicated to specific tasks or activities. By pre-scheduling your time, you eliminate decision fatigue and provide your brain with clear expectations about what to focus on.

How to Implement Time-Blocking:

1. **List Your Priorities**: Identify the tasks that need to be completed for the day.
2. **Assign Time Blocks**: Allocate a specific time period for each task. For example, 9:00–10:00 AM for writing, 10:00–10:30 AM for emails.
3. **Include Breaks**: Schedule short breaks between blocks to recharge and prevent burnout.
4. **Stick to the Schedule**: Treat your time blocks as non-negotiable appointments.

By using time-blocking, you create structure in your day, making it easier to stay focused and productive.

2. The Pomodoro Method

The Pomodoro Technique is a time management system designed to boost focus and productivity by breaking work into manageable intervals. Developed by Francesco Cirillo, this method is named after the tomato-shaped timer he used while studying.

How to Use the Pomodoro Technique:

1. **Choose a Task**: Select one task to work on.
2. **Set a Timer**: Set a timer for 25 minutes (one "Pomodoro").
3. **Work Intensely**: Focus solely on the task until the timer rings.
4. **Take a Short Break**: Rest for 5 minutes.
5. **Repeat**: After completing four Pomodoros, take a longer break (15–30 minutes).

This technique trains your brain to focus in short bursts while incorporating regular breaks to prevent mental fatigue.

3. Mindfulness Practices

Mindfulness is the practice of bringing your attention to the present moment without judgment. It strengthens the brain's ability to concentrate and reduces the impact of distractions.

Mindfulness Techniques for Focus:

- **Breath Awareness**: Spend 2–5 minutes focusing on your breath. When your mind wanders, gently redirect it to your breathing.
- **Body Scans**: Close your eyes and mentally scan your body, noticing areas of tension. This exercise promotes relaxation and sharpens awareness.
- **Mindful Observation**: Choose an object nearby (e.g., a plant or a pen) and study it for a minute. Notice its color, texture, and details. This trains your attention to stay in the moment.

Practicing mindfulness regularly enhances your overall ability to concentrate and stay present.

Strategies for Creating a Distraction-Free Environment

Your surroundings significantly impact your ability to focus. By intentionally designing your workspace, you can minimize distractions and create an environment that supports concentration.

1. Declutter Your Space

A cluttered environment can lead to a cluttered mind. Remove unnecessary items from your workspace and keep it organized. A clean desk signals to your brain that it's time to work.

2. Use Noise Management Tools

- **Noise-Canceling Headphones**: Block out external distractions with noise-canceling headphones or earplugs.
- **Ambient Noise Apps**: Use apps like Noisli or Calm to play background sounds that promote focus, such as white noise or nature sounds.

3. Turn Off Notifications

Digital interruptions are one of the biggest barriers to focus. Turn off non-essential notifications on your phone, email, and apps during work periods.

4. Set Boundaries

Communicate with those around you about your need for uninterrupted time. Use visual signals, such as a "Do Not Disturb" sign, to let others know you're focusing.

5. Control Your Digital Environment

- **Website Blockers**: Use tools like Freedom or StayFocusd to block distracting websites.
- **Focus-Only Devices**: Consider using a minimalist device, such as a digital typewriter or distraction-free writing app.

Quick Routines for Boosting Mental Energy and Sharpening Attention

Mental energy and sharp attention are prerequisites for focus. Incorporating quick routines into your day can help refresh your mind and improve your ability to concentrate.

1. The 5-Minute Energy Booster

- Stand up and stretch your arms, legs, and back to release tension.
- Perform light exercises, such as jumping jacks or walking in place, to increase blood flow.
- Take 5 deep breaths, inhaling deeply through your nose and exhaling slowly through your mouth.

2. The Hydration and Nutrition Reset

Dehydration and low blood sugar can hinder focus. Keep a water bottle at your desk and sip throughout the day. Snack on brain-boosting foods like nuts, seeds, or dark chocolate.

3. The Micro-Meditation

Close your eyes and take 10 slow, deep breaths. Focus on the sensation of air entering and leaving your nostrils. This quick meditation calms the mind and resets your attention.

4. The Eye Break

Staring at a screen for long periods can strain your eyes and sap your focus. Follow the **20-20-20 rule**: every 20 minutes, look at an object 20 feet away for 20 seconds.

Conclusion

Building a focus toolkit is about equipping yourself with strategies that work for your unique needs and lifestyle. Time-blocking, the Pomodoro Method, and mindfulness practices provide foundational techniques to enhance your attention, while creating a distraction-free environment sets the stage for success. Finally, incorporating quick routines into your day keeps your mental energy sharp and your focus strong.

With these tools in hand, you're ready to tackle distractions and maintain concentration like never before. In the next chapter, we'll delve deeper into the Instant Focus Formula and explore how to seamlessly integrate these techniques into your daily life.

Chapter 3: Reclaiming Your Attention in a Distracted World

In a world where distractions are abundant and attention is constantly pulled in different directions, reclaiming control over your focus has never been more essential. The key to mastering focus lies in recognizing and eliminating the "attention thieves" that disrupt your mental clarity, decluttering your environment to create a space conducive to productivity, and effectively managing your tasks and energy. In this chapter, we'll explore actionable steps to help you reclaim your attention and take charge of your day.

Identifying and Eliminating Attention Thieves

Attention thieves are habits, tools, and distractions that subtly rob you of the focus you need to thrive. Identifying these culprits is the first step in regaining control.

Common Attention Thieves

1. **Unnecessary Notifications**
   - Notifications from social media, emails, and apps constantly demand attention, interrupting your train of thought and fragmenting your focus.
2. **Multitasking**
   - Trying to juggle multiple tasks simultaneously creates cognitive overload, reducing efficiency and increasing mistakes.
3. **Open Tabs and Devices**
   - Keeping multiple browser tabs, apps, or devices open creates visual clutter and encourages task-switching.
4. **Constant Connectivity**
   - The pressure to stay connected and respond immediately to messages or calls disrupts deep work and mental flow.

5. Emotional Distractions

- Stress, anxiety, or unresolved conflicts occupy mental space, making it harder to concentrate.

Steps to Eliminate Attention Thieves

1. Audit Your Notifications

- Go through your phone, email, and apps. Turn off all non-essential notifications.
- Use "Do Not Disturb" mode during work hours to minimize interruptions.

2. Ban Multitasking

- Focus on one task at a time. Use techniques like the Pomodoro Method (discussed in Chapter 2) to structure your work into manageable intervals.

3. Close Tabs and Simplify Tools

- Limit yourself to one or two open tabs or apps at a time.
- Use specialized tools or apps designed for focused work, such as Notion or Todoist.

4. Schedule Connectivity

- Set specific times for checking emails, messages, and social media.
- Let colleagues and loved ones know your availability to manage expectations.

5. Address Emotional Distractions

- Dedicate time to resolve issues or practice mindfulness to manage stress and anxiety.

Decluttering Your Digital and Physical Spaces

Your environment plays a crucial role in your ability to focus. A cluttered space, whether digital or physical, creates mental noise that competes for your attention.

Decluttering Digital Spaces

1. **Organize Your Desktop**
   - Create a minimalist desktop with only essential folders visible.
   - Use a simple background to reduce visual distractions.
2. **Streamline Your Email**
   - Unsubscribe from unnecessary newsletters and promotional emails.
   - Use filters to sort messages into categories automatically.
3. **Curate Your Apps**
   - Delete unused apps from your phone and computer.
   - Rearrange your home screen to prioritize tools that help you focus.
4. **Declutter Social Media**
   - Unfollow accounts that don't add value to your life.
   - Limit your time on social media using timers or app blockers.

Decluttering Physical Spaces

1. **Clear Your Desk**
   - Remove everything except the essentials: your computer, notebook, pen, and a drink.
   - Store non-essential items in drawers or shelves.
2. **Create Zones**
   - Dedicate specific areas for work, relaxation, and other activities. This helps your brain associate each zone with its purpose.
3. **Optimize Lighting**
   - Use natural light or desk lamps to create a well-lit workspace that minimizes eye strain.
4. **Add Focus-Friendly Elements**
   - Incorporate plants, calming artwork, or a vision board to create an environment that inspires productivity.

Prioritizing Tasks and Managing Energy

Reclaiming your attention isn't just about eliminating distractions—it's about ensuring that your energy is channeled toward the tasks that truly matter. Prioritization and energy management are critical to staying focused and achieving your goals.

Prioritizing Tasks

1. **The Eisenhower Matrix**
   - Divide your tasks into four categories:
     - **Urgent and Important**: Do these immediately.
     - **Important but Not Urgent**: Schedule these for later.
     - **Urgent but Not Important**: Delegate these tasks if possible.
     - **Neither Urgent nor Important**: Eliminate these tasks.
2. **Identify Your Most Important Tasks (MITs)**
   - Start each day by identifying 1–3 MITs. These are the tasks that will have the greatest impact on your goals.
3. **Batch Similar Tasks**
   - Group similar activities, like responding to emails or making phone calls, and complete them in one focused session.

Managing Energy

1. **Work with Your Energy Levels**
   - Identify your peak productivity times (e.g., morning, afternoon) and schedule your most demanding tasks during these periods.
2. **Take Breaks**
   - Use techniques like the Pomodoro Method to incorporate regular breaks, allowing your brain to recharge.
3. **Stay Hydrated and Eat Smart**
   - Fuel your brain with water and nutrient-dense snacks like fruits, nuts, and whole grains.
4. **Move Your Body**
   - Incorporate light physical activity, such as stretching or a short walk, to boost energy and combat fatigue.
5. **Prioritize Sleep**
   - Aim for 7–8 hours of quality sleep each night to ensure your brain functions at its best.

Conclusion

Reclaiming your attention in a distracted world requires a deliberate and consistent effort to identify and eliminate attention thieves, declutter your spaces, and manage your tasks and energy effectively. By taking these steps, you can create an environment that supports focus, clarity, and productivity.

With these strategies in place, you are better equipped to integrate the Instant Focus Formula into your daily life. In the next chapter, we'll explore how to build and sustain focus habits that last, ensuring your ability to stay sharp and present in any situation.

Chapter 4: The Instant Focus Formula in Action

Now that you've gained a foundational understanding of focus and built a toolkit for enhancing attention, it's time to put everything into practice. The **Instant Focus Formula** is a simple, repeatable system designed to help you cut through distractions and direct your attention to what matters most. In this chapter, we'll break down the formula into actionable steps, provide real-world examples for various scenarios, and offer troubleshooting tips for overcoming common focus challenges.

Breaking Down the Instant Focus Formula

The Instant Focus Formula is built around three key principles: **Prepare**, **Engage**, and **Reflect**. By following these steps, you'll create a structure for your focus sessions, maximize productivity, and continually improve your ability to concentrate.

Step 1: Prepare

Before diving into any task, preparation is essential. A clear mind and an organized workspace set the stage for effective focus.

1. **Define Your Goal**
   - Be specific about what you want to achieve in the focus session.
   - Example: Instead of saying, "I'll work on my project," say, "I'll write the introduction to my project report."
2. **Set a Time Limit**
   - Choose a realistic timeframe for your session (e.g., 25 minutes using the Pomodoro Technique or 90 minutes for deep work).
3. **Eliminate Distractions**
   - Turn off notifications, close unnecessary tabs, and inform others not to disturb you.
4. **Gather Your Tools**
   - Have all the materials you need within arm's reach to avoid interruptions.

Step 2: Engage

This is the action phase, where you fully immerse yourself in the task at hand.

1. **Start with Intention**
   - Take a deep breath, remind yourself of your goal, and begin.
2. **Use a Focus Method**
   - Employ techniques like time-blocking, the Pomodoro Technique, or mindfulness to structure your session.
3. **Stay Single-Tasked**
   - Commit to working on one task without switching to another.
   - If distractions arise, write them down to address later, and refocus on your task.
4. **Monitor Your Attention**
   - Notice when your mind starts to wander and gently bring it back to your work.

Step 3: Reflect

Reflection is a crucial but often overlooked part of the focus process. It allows you to evaluate your performance and make improvements for future sessions.

1. **Review Your Progress**
   - At the end of the session, assess whether you achieved your goal.
2. **Celebrate Small Wins**
   - Acknowledge what you accomplished, no matter how small. This reinforces positive focus habits.
3. **Identify Challenges**
   - Note any distractions or obstacles you encountered and think about how to address them next time.

4. **Plan Your Next Session**
   ◦ Use what you learned to prepare for your next focus session, making adjustments as needed.

Applying the Instant Focus Formula

The formula is versatile and can be applied to a variety of situations, from professional work to personal projects. Let's look at how it works in different contexts.

1. Applying the Formula at Work

Scenario: Writing a Quarterly Report

- **Prepare**: Clear your desk, close email tabs, and define your goal: "Draft the executive summary."
- **Engage**: Set a timer for 90 minutes, use a Pomodoro timer for breaks, and focus solely on writing.
- **Reflect**: Review your draft, note sections that need more research, and schedule a follow-up session.

2. Applying the Formula in Study

Scenario: Preparing for an Exam

- **Prepare**: Organize your study materials, set a goal: "Review chapters 3 and 4," and silence your phone.
- **Engage**: Use the Pomodoro Technique (25 minutes of study, 5-minute breaks), and quiz yourself at the end of each interval.
- **Reflect**: Assess which topics you mastered and which need more attention, and plan additional study sessions.

3. Applying the Formula to Personal Projects

Scenario: Learning a New Skill (e.g., Guitar Practice)

- **Prepare**: Define your goal: "Learn and practice the A minor chord transitions," and ensure your guitar and tuner are ready.

- **Engage**: Set a 30-minute timer, focus on practicing the chord changes, and avoid checking your phone.
- **Reflect**: Record your progress, note any challenges (e.g., difficulty transitioning between chords), and plan to address them next session.

Troubleshooting Common Focus Challenges

Even with the best intentions, you may encounter challenges while using the Instant Focus Formula. Here's how to overcome them.

Challenge 1: Mental Fatigue
Solution:

- Break tasks into smaller chunks to make them more manageable.
- Incorporate quick energy-boosting routines, such as a 5-minute walk or deep breathing.

Challenge 2: Persistent Distractions
Solution:

- Use noise-canceling headphones or work in a distraction-free environment.
- Implement digital tools like website blockers to minimize online temptations.

Challenge 3: Difficulty Getting Started
Solution:

- Use the "2-Minute Rule": Commit to working on a task for just two minutes. Often, this small start is enough to build momentum.
- Create a ritual to signal the start of a focus session, such as lighting a candle or taking a deep breath.

Challenge 4: Losing Focus Mid-Session
Solution:

- Pause and perform a quick mindfulness exercise, such as focusing on your breath for one minute.
- Write down the distraction to address later, then redirect your attention to the task.

Challenge 5: Feeling Overwhelmed by the Task
Solution:

- Break the task into smaller, more specific steps.
- Use time-blocking to work on just one step at a time.

Conclusion

The Instant Focus Formula is a practical, adaptable method that can be applied to any area of your life where focus is required. By following the steps to **Prepare**, **Engage**, and **Reflect**, you can harness your attention and achieve meaningful progress toward your goals. With practice and persistence, this formula will become a cornerstone of your productivity and well-being.

Chapter 5: Sustaining Focus Over Time

Mastering focus is not about achieving short-term bursts of productivity; it's about cultivating a sustainable habit that serves you over the long term. Maintaining focus over time requires consistent effort, intentionality, and a recognition of the importance of balance. This chapter explores the strategies and mindset shifts necessary to make focus a lasting part of your life, including the role of rest, recovery, and self-compassion in avoiding burnout. Additionally, we'll draw inspiration from real-life stories of individuals who have successfully transformed their productivity through focused practices.

Building and Sustaining Focus Habits

1. Consistency Over Perfection

Creating a long-term habit of focus doesn't mean achieving flawless attention every day. Instead, the goal is to build a routine that supports your ability to focus consistently.

Strategies:

- **Anchor Your Focus Practice**: Tie your focus sessions to existing habits. For example, start a work session right after your morning coffee or meditation.
- **Start Small**: Commit to short, manageable focus sessions initially, then gradually increase their length as your capacity grows.
- **Track Your Progress**: Use a journal or app to log your focus sessions. This creates a sense of accountability and highlights improvements over time.

2. Adopt a Growth Mindset

Embrace the idea that focus is a skill that can be developed with practice. Mistakes and setbacks are part of the learning process.

Strategies:

- **Reflect and Adapt**: After a difficult focus session, ask yourself what worked and what didn't, then adjust accordingly.
- **Celebrate Small Wins**: Acknowledge even minor progress, such as resisting the urge to check your phone during a session.

3. Set Long-Term Goals

Having clear, meaningful goals provides direction for your focus efforts and keeps you motivated.

Strategies:

- **Break Goals into Milestones**: Divide larger objectives into smaller, actionable steps to maintain momentum.
- **Visualize Success**: Spend a few minutes each day picturing what achieving your goals will feel like. This reinforces your commitment to staying focused.

The Role of Rest, Recovery, and Self-Compassion

Maintaining focus over time requires more than discipline—it also depends on how well you balance work with rest and recovery. Without this balance, burnout becomes a real risk.

1. Prioritize Rest

Rest is not a luxury; it's a necessity for sustained focus. Your brain needs time to recover and consolidate information.

Types of Rest:

- **Physical Rest**: Adequate sleep (7–8 hours per night) is essential for mental clarity and cognitive function.
- **Mental Rest**: Take short breaks throughout the day to recharge your mind.
- **Sensory Rest**: Reduce exposure to screens, loud environments, and other overstimulating inputs.

2. Incorporate Recovery Practices

Intentional recovery activities help your brain reset and prepare for future focus sessions.

Practices:

- **Mindfulness Meditation**: Even a few minutes of mindfulness each day can reduce stress and enhance your ability to focus.
- **Exercise**: Physical activity improves blood flow to the brain, boosting cognitive performance.
- **Creative Hobbies**: Engaging in creative activities like painting or playing music allows your brain to recharge while fostering innovation.

3. Practice Self-Compassion

No one maintains perfect focus all the time. When you encounter distractions or setbacks, treat yourself with kindness instead of criticism.

Strategies:

- **Reframe Mistakes**: View distractions as opportunities to learn and improve rather than failures.
- **Speak Kindly to Yourself**: Use encouraging language, such as, "It's okay—I'll try again," instead of harsh self-criticism.
- **Rest Without Guilt**: Recognize that downtime is essential and doesn't make you "lazy" or unproductive.

Inspiring Stories of Transformation

Sometimes, hearing how others have overcome challenges and mastered focus can reignite your motivation. Here are a few stories of individuals who turned their lives around with focused practices.

1. The Writer Who Battled Procrastination

Samantha, a freelance writer, struggled to complete her articles on time due to endless distractions from social media and email. Frustrated by missed deadlines, she decided to implement the **Pomodoro Technique** and dedicate specific hours to writing without interruptions. Over time, Samantha's productivity skyrocketed, allowing her to take on more clients and even publish her first book. Her secret? Consistency and a commitment to staying single-tasked.

2. The Entrepreneur Who Overcame Burnout

David, a startup founder, was juggling multiple roles and working 14-hour days, which left him exhausted and unfocused. After experiencing burnout, he restructured his schedule to include regular breaks, exercise, and mindfulness meditation. He also began using time-blocking to allocate focused periods for deep work. Within months, David not only regained his productivity but also found a better work-life balance, leading to the successful launch of his company's flagship product.

3. The Student Who Mastered Exam Prep

Maria, a university student, often felt overwhelmed by the sheer amount of material she needed to study. She adopted the **Instant Focus Formula**, breaking her study sessions into manageable intervals and eliminating distractions during her study blocks. She also started reflecting on her progress after each session, adjusting her methods as needed. The result? Maria's grades improved dramatically, and she graduated with honors.

Conclusion

Sustaining focus over time is about building habits, balancing effort with rest, and approaching your practice with patience and self-compassion. By implementing strategies for consistency, incorporating recovery practices, and learning from inspiring examples, you can make focus a permanent and transformative part of your life.

In the next chapter, we'll explore advanced strategies for focus mastery, including using technology wisely and leveraging the science of habit formation to reinforce your focus practices even further. Let's continue this journey toward unparalleled attention and productivity!

Appendix A: 10 Quick Focus Boosters

Sometimes, despite our best efforts, distractions creep in and derail our concentration. Whether you're mid-task or preparing to begin, these quick focus boosters can help you regain clarity and momentum. Each technique is designed to be simple, effective, and actionable, taking no more than a few minutes to implement.

1. The 4-7-8 Breathing Technique

Deep breathing is one of the fastest ways to calm the mind and restore focus. The 4-7-8 method helps regulate your nervous system, reducing stress and sharpening attention.

How to Do It:

1. Inhale deeply through your nose for **4 seconds.**
2. Hold your breath for **7 seconds.**
3. Exhale slowly and completely through your mouth for **8 seconds**.
4. Repeat 3–4 times.

Why It Works:

This technique increases oxygen flow to the brain, lowers heart rate, and shifts your focus inward.

2. The 5-Second Reset

This quick mental exercise clears the clutter in your mind and recenters your attention.

How to Do It:

1. Close your eyes.
2. Count slowly from 1 to 5, visualizing each number as you say it.
3. At the end, take a deep breath and open your eyes.

Why It Works:

By temporarily pausing and redirecting your attention, this exercise helps you "reset" your mental state.

3. Visualization Focus Primer

Visualization harnesses the power of your imagination to guide your mind toward clarity and purpose.

How to Do It:

1. Close your eyes and visualize yourself successfully completing the task you're working on.
2. Imagine the steps you'll take, how you'll feel when it's done, and the sense of accomplishment.
3. Open your eyes and begin your task with this mental image in mind.

Why It Works:

Visualization creates a sense of purpose and motivation, helping you align your thoughts with your goals.

4. The 3-2-1 Grounding Technique

Grounding techniques anchor you in the present moment, cutting through mental distractions.

How to Do It:

1. Identify **3 things you can see** around you.
2. Name **2 things you can touch** and briefly feel their texture.
3. Focus on **1 thing you can hear**, like the hum of a fan or birds outside.

Why It Works:

This technique engages your senses and redirects your mind to the here and now, clearing distractions.

5. Mini Meditation

A short meditation session can work wonders for your focus and clarity.

How to Do It:

1. Sit comfortably, close your eyes, and take a deep breath.
2. Focus on your breath as it moves in and out.
3. If your mind wanders, gently bring your attention back to your breath.
4. Practice for 2–3 minutes.

Why It Works:

Meditation reduces mental noise, enhances awareness, and improves your ability to concentrate.

6. The Body Scan

Physical tension can subtly undermine your ability to focus. A body scan helps release it quickly.

How to Do It:

1. Close your eyes and take a deep breath.
2. Starting at the top of your head, slowly scan down your body, noticing any tension.
3. When you identify tension, consciously relax that area.
4. Continue until you reach your toes.

Why It Works:

By releasing physical tension, you free up mental energy for focus.

7. Micro-Movement Break

Physical activity, even in small doses, can refresh your mind and boost your energy.

How to Do It:

1. Stand up and stretch your arms overhead.
2. Perform 10 jumping jacks or jog in place for 30 seconds.
3. Shake out your hands and arms before sitting back down.

Why It Works:

Movement increases blood flow and oxygen to the brain, improving alertness and concentration.

8. Task Re-Engagement

When focus slips, reconnecting with your task in a structured way can help.

How to Do It:

1. Pause and restate the purpose of the task you're working on.
2. Break the task into smaller steps if it feels overwhelming.
3. Commit to completing just one small step before reassessing.

Why It Works:

This method reduces overwhelm and helps you rebuild momentum by focusing on manageable actions.

9. Cold Water Refresh

A splash of cold water can provide an instant wake-up for your mind and body.

How to Do It:

1. Go to the sink and splash cold water on your face.
2. Pat your face dry and take a deep breath.
3. Return to your task feeling refreshed.

Why It Works:

The cold water stimulates your nervous system and boosts alertness, helping you shake off sluggishness.

10. The Gratitude Shift

Gratitude helps shift your mindset from distraction or frustration to positivity and clarity.

How to Do It:

1. Pause and think of three things you're grateful for in this moment.
2. Write them down if possible or say them out loud.
3. Take a deep breath and return to your task with a lighter mindset.

Why It Works:

Focusing on gratitude reduces stress and negativity, creating a mental environment more conducive to focus.

Conclusion

These 10 quick focus boosters are your go-to tools for regaining clarity and concentration whenever distractions threaten to derail your efforts. By incorporating one or more of these techniques into your routine, you'll develop the ability to reset your focus instantly and stay on track no matter what challenges arise. Keep this list handy as a resource to help you stay productive and intentional in your work and daily life.

Appendix B: Focus Resources and Tools

Enhancing your focus is a journey that can be greatly supported by the right resources and tools. This appendix provides a curated list of recommended apps, books, and productivity tools designed to help you stay on track. Additionally, we've included printable templates for task prioritization, time-blocking, and focus habit tracking to aid in your daily practice.

Recommended Apps and Digital Tools

In the digital age, technology can both hinder and help our ability to focus. The following apps are designed to minimize distractions, organize tasks, and promote mindfulness, turning your devices into allies rather than adversaries.

Focus Enhancement Apps

1. **Forest**
   - **Description**: Forest gamifies focus by allowing you to grow virtual trees as you stay away from your phone. If you leave the app, your tree withers.
   - **Features**: Task timer, focus statistics, and the ability to plant real trees through partnered organizations.

2. **Freedom**
   - **Description**: Freedom blocks distracting websites and apps across all your devices.
   - **Features**: Customizable block lists, scheduling of focus sessions, and lockdown mode for serious concentration.

3. **Cold Turkey**
   - **Description**: A powerful website and application blocker for your computer.
   - **Features**: Scheduled blocks, frozen turkey mode (can't be undone), and the ability to block the entire internet if needed.

Task Management Apps

1. Todoist
- **Description**: A versatile task management app that helps you organize tasks, set priorities, and track progress.
- **Features**: Recurring due dates, project sections, labels, filters, and productivity tracking.

2. Trello
- **Description**: A visual project management tool that uses boards, lists, and cards to organize tasks.
- **Features**: Drag-and-drop interface, collaboration tools, and integrations with other apps.

3. Notion
- **Description**: An all-in-one workspace for notes, tasks, wikis, and databases.
- **Features**: Customizable templates, team collaboration, and the ability to integrate different content types in one place.

Time Management and Focus Timing Apps

1. Pomodoro Timer Apps
- **Description**: Apps like **Focus Keeper** or **Pomodoro Tracker** help implement the Pomodoro Technique.
- **Features**: Customizable work and break intervals, session tracking, and productivity reports.

2. RescueTime
- **Description**: Tracks your digital activities to provide insights into how you spend your time.
- **Features**: Automatic time tracking, goal setting, distraction blocking, and detailed reports.

Mindfulness and Relaxation Apps

1. Headspace
- **Description**: A meditation app with guided sessions to improve mindfulness and reduce stress.
- **Features**: Meditation exercises, sleep aids, focus music, and mindfulness reminders.

2. Calm
- **Description**: Offers guided meditations, sleep stories, and relaxing music to enhance focus and well-being.
- **Features**: Daily meditation sessions, breathing exercises, and a variety of soothing sounds.

Recommended Books and Reading Resources

Books offer in-depth insights and strategies for mastering focus, productivity, and personal development. The following titles are highly regarded for their practical advice and engaging content.

On Focus and Deep Work

1. **"Deep Work: Rules for Focused Success in a Distracted World" by Cal Newport**
   - **Overview**: Explores the value of deep, undistracted work and provides strategies to cultivate focus in a noisy world.
2. **"Indistractable: How to Control Your Attention and Choose Your Life" by Nir Eyal**
   - **Overview**: Offers a framework for understanding and overcoming distractions to become indistractable.
3. **"The One Thing: The Surprisingly Simple Truth Behind Extraordinary Results" by Gary Keller and Jay Papasan**
   - **Overview**: Emphasizes the importance of focusing on one key task at a time to achieve significant results.

On Habits and Productivity

1. **"Atomic Habits: An Easy & Proven Way to Build Good Habits & Break Bad Ones" by James Clear**
   - **Overview**: Provides practical strategies for habit formation to improve focus and productivity.
2. **"The Power of Habit: Why We Do What We Do in Life and Business" by Charles Duhigg**
   - **Overview**: Explores the science behind habit formation and how to leverage it for personal and professional growth.
3. **"Essentialism: The Disciplined Pursuit of Less" by Greg McKeown**
   - **Overview**: Encourages focusing on what is truly essential and eliminating the non-essential to improve effectiveness.

On Mindfulness and Well-being

1. **"Mindfulness in Plain English" by Bhante Henepola Gunaratana**
   - **Overview**: A clear guide to mindfulness meditation practices that enhance focus and reduce stress.
2. **"Wherever You Go, There You Are" by Jon Kabat-Zinn**
   - **Overview**: Introduces mindfulness meditation in everyday life to cultivate presence and attention.

Productivity Tools and Accessories

Sometimes, the right physical tools can make a significant difference in your ability to focus and stay organized.

Analog Tools

1. **Bullet Journal**
   - **Description**: A customizable journaling system that uses bullet points and symbols to track tasks, events, and notes.
   - **Benefits**: Enhances organization, prioritizes tasks, and provides a creative outlet.
2. **Planner Notebooks**
   - **Recommendations**:
     - **The Full Focus Planner**: Integrates goal setting with daily task management.
     - **Passion Planner**: Combines personal and professional planning with reflection prompts.
3. **Whiteboards and Sticky Notes**
   - **Uses**: Visualize tasks, brainstorm ideas, and keep important reminders in sight.

Ergonomic Accessories

1. **Standing Desks**
   - **Benefits**: Promote better posture, increase energy levels, and can enhance focus.
2. **Blue Light Blocking Glasses**
   - **Benefits**: Reduce eye strain from screens, helping maintain focus during long work sessions.
3. **Noise-Canceling Headphones**

- Recommendations:
    - **Bose QuietComfort Series**
    - **Sony WH-1000XM Series**
- **Benefits**: Block out ambient noise, allowing for a distraction-free environment.

Printable Templates

To support your focus journey, we've included printable templates that you can customize and use daily. These templates are designed to help you prioritize tasks, schedule your time effectively, and track your focus habits.

1. Task Prioritization Templates
Eisenhower Matrix Template

- **Description**: Helps categorize tasks based on urgency and importance, allowing you to decide what to do, schedule, delegate, or eliminate.
- **How to Use**:
    1. **Urgent and Important**: Do these tasks immediately.
    2. **Important but Not Urgent**: Schedule these tasks.
    3. **Urgent but Not Important**: Delegate if possible.
    4. **Neither Urgent nor Important**: Consider eliminating these tasks.

Daily Priority Planner

- **Description**: A template to list your top 3–5 priorities for the day, ensuring focus on what matters most.
- **Features**:
    - Sections for Must-Do Tasks, Should-Do Tasks, and Nice-to-Do Tasks.
    - Space for notes and reflections.

2. Time-Blocking Templates
Weekly Time-Blocking Schedule

- **Description**: A calendar layout where you can block out time slots for specific tasks and activities throughout the week.
- **How to Use**:
  1. Fill in fixed commitments (meetings, appointments).
  2. Allocate blocks for high-priority tasks.
  3. Include time for breaks, exercise, and personal activities.

Daily Time-Blocking Sheet

- **Description**: A detailed daily planner broken down into hourly segments.
- **Features**:
  - Time slots from early morning to evening.
  - Sections for notes and to-dos.
  - Checkboxes to mark completed tasks.

3. Focus Habit Tracker
Monthly Focus Habit Tracker

- **Description**: A calendar grid to track your focus habits over a month.
- **How to Use**:
  1. Define the habits you want to build (e.g., "30 minutes of meditation," "No phone during work sessions").
  2. Mark each day you successfully complete the habit.
  3. Review at the end of the month to assess your consistency.

Focus Session Log

- **Description**: A template to record individual focus sessions.

- **Features**:
  - ◦ Sections for Date, Start and End Time, Goal for the Session.
  - ◦ Space to note Distractions Encountered and Strategies Used.
  - ◦ Reflection prompts like "What went well?" and "What can I improve?"

How to Access and Use the Templates

1. **Printing**: The templates are designed for standard A4 or letter-sized paper. Print multiple copies as needed.
2. **Customization**: Feel free to adjust the templates to suit your preferences. You can add sections, change layouts, or integrate them into digital note-taking apps.
3. **Consistency**: Incorporate these templates into your daily routine to maximize their effectiveness. Regular use will help reinforce focus habits and improve productivity.

Conclusion

Equipping yourself with the right resources and tools can significantly enhance your ability to focus and achieve your goals. Whether it's leveraging technology through apps, gaining insights from thought-provoking books, utilizing physical productivity tools, or organizing your tasks with printable templates, each resource contributes to building a robust focus practice.

Remember, the journey to mastering focus is personal and ongoing. Experiment with different tools and techniques to discover what resonates with you. Stay curious, stay committed, and let these resources support you on your path to greater productivity and fulfillment.

<u>Message from the Author:</u>

I hope you enjoyed this book, I love astrology and knew there was not a book such as this out on the shelf. I love metaphysical items as well. Please check out my other books:

-Life of Government Benefits

-My life of Hell

-My life with Hydrocephalus

-Red Sky

-World Domination:Woman's rule

-World Domination:Woman's Rule 2: The War

-Life and Banishment of Apophis: book 1

-The Kidney Friendly Diet

-The Ultimate Hemp Cookbook

-Creating a Dispensary(legally)

-Cleanliness throughout life: the importance of showering from childhood to adulthood.

-Strong Roots: The Risks of Overcoddling children

-Hemp Horoscopes: Cosmic Insights and Earthly Healing

- Celestial Hemp Navigating the Zodiac: Through the Green Cosmos

-Astrological Hemp: Aligning The Stars with Earth's Ancient Herb

-The Astrological Guide to Hemp: Stars, Signs, and Sacred Leaves

-Green Growth: Innovative Marketing Strategies for your Hemp Products and Dispensary

-Cosmic Cannabis

-Astrological Munchies

-Henry The Hemp

-Zodiacal Roots: The Astrological Soul Of Hemp

- **Green Constellations: Intersection of Hemp and Zodiac**

-Hemp in The Houses: An astrological Adventure Through The Cannabis Galaxy

-Galactic Ganja Guide

Heavenly Hemp

Zodiac Leaves

Doctor Who Astrology

Cannastrology

Stellar Satvias and Cosmic Indicas

Celestial Cannabis: A Zodiac Journey

AstroHerbology: The Sky and The Soil: Volume 1

AstroHerbology:Celestial Cannabis:Volume 2

Cosmic Cannabis Cultivation

The Starry Guide to Herbal Harmony: Volume 1

The Starry Guide to Herbal Harmony: Cannabis Universe: Volume 2

Yugioh Astrology: Astrological Guide to Deck, Duels and more

Nightmare Mansion: Echoes of The Abyss

Nightmare Mansion 2: Legacy of Shadows

Nightmare Mansion 3: Shadows of the Forgotten

Nightmare Mansion 4: Echoes of the Damned

The Life and Banishment of Apophis: Book 2

Nightmare Mansion: Halls of Despair

Healing with Herb: Cannabis and Hydrocephalus

Planetary Pot: Aligning with Astrological Herbs: Volume 1

Fast Track to Freedom: 30 Days to Financial Independence Using AI, Assets, and Agile Hustles

Cosmic Hemp Pathways

How to Become Financially Free in 30 Days: 10,000 Paths to Prosperity

Zodiacal Herbage: Astrological Insights: Volume 1

Nightmare Mansion: Whispers in the Walls

The Daleks Invade Atlantis

Henry the hemp and Hydrocephalus

10X The Kidney Friendly Diet

Cannabis Universe: Adult coloring book

Hemp Astrology: The Healing Power of the Stars

Zodiacal Herbage: Astrological Insights: Cannabis Universe: Volume 2

<u>Planetary Pot: Aligning with Astrological Herbs: Cannabis Universes: Volume 2</u>

Doctor Who Meets the Replicators and SG-1: The Ultimate Battle for Survival

Nightmare Mansion: Curse of the Blood Moon

<u>The Celestial Stoner: A Guide to the Zodiac</u>

Cosmic Pleasures: Sex Toy Astrology for Every Sign

Hydrocephalus Astrology: Navigating the Stars and Healing Waters

Lapis and the Mischievous Chocolate Bar

Celestial Positions: Sexual Astrology for Every Sign

Apophis's Shadow Work Journal: : A Journey of Self-Discovery and Healing

Kinky Cosmos: Sexual Kink Astrology for Every Sign

Digital Cosmos: The Astrological Digimon Compendium

Stellar Seeds: The Cosmic Guide to Growing with Astrology

Apophis's Daily Gratitude Journal

Cat Astrology: Feline Mysteries of the Cosmos

The Cosmic Kama Sutra: An Astrological Guide to Sexual Positions

Unleash Your Potential: A Guided Journal Powered by AI Insights

Whispers of the Enchanted Grove

Cosmic Pleasures: An Astrological Guide to Sexual Kinks

369, 12 Manifestation Journal

Whisper of the nocturne journal(blank journal for writing or drawing)

The Boogey Book

Locked In Reflection: A Chastity Journey Through Locktober

Generating Wealth Quickly:

How to Generate $100,000 in 24 Hours

Star Magic: Harness the Power of the Universe

The Flatulence Chronicles: A Fart Journal for Self-Discovery

The Doctor and The Death Moth

Seize the Day: A Personal Seizure Tracking Journal

The Ultimate Boogeyman Safari: A Journey into the Boogie World and Beyond

Whispers of Samhain: 1,000 Spells of Love, Luck, and Lunar Magic: Samhain Spell Book

Apophis's guides:

Witch's Spellbook Crafting Guide for Halloween

<u>Frost & Flame: The Enchanted Yule Grimoire of 1000 Winter Spells</u>

<u>The Ultimate Boogey Goo Guide & Spooky Activities for Halloween Fun</u>

Harmony of the Scales: A Libra's Spellcraft for Balance and Beauty

The Enchanted Advent: 36 Days of Christmas Wonders

Nightmare Mansion: The Labyrinth of Screams

Harvest of Enchantment: 1,000 Spells of Gratitude, Love, and Fortune for Thanksgiving

The Boogey Chronicles: A Journal of Nightly Encounters and Shadowy Secrets

The 12 Days of Financial Freedom: A Step-by-Step Christmas Countdown to Transform Your Finances

Sigil of the Eternal Spiral Blank Journal

A Christmas Feast: Timeless Recipes for Every Meal

Cosmic Sales: The Astrological Guide to Black Friday Shopping
Legends of the Corn Mother and Other Harvest Myths
Whispers of the Harvest: The Corn Mother's Journal
The Evergreen Spellbook
The Doctor Meets the Boogeyman
The White Witch of Rose Hall's SpellBook
The Gingerbread Golem's Shadow: A Study in Sweet Darkness
The Gingerbread Golem Codex: An Academic Exploration of Sweet Myths
The Gingerbread Golem Grimoire: Sweet Magicks and Spells for the Festive Witch
The Curse of the Gingerbread Golem
10-minute Christmas Crafts for kids
<u>Christmas Crisis Solutions: The Ultimate Last-Minute Survival Guide</u>
Gingerbread Golem Recipes: Holiday Treats with a Magical Twist
The Infinite Key: Unlocking Mystical Secrets of the Ages
Enchanted Yule: A Wiccan and Pagan Guide to a Magical and Memorable Season
Dinosaurs of Power: Unlocking Ancient Magick
Astro-Dinos: The Cosmic Guide to Prehistoric Wisdom
Gallifrey's Yule Logs: A Festive Doctor Who Cookbook
The Dino Grimoire: Secrets of Prehistoric Magick
The Gift They Never Knew They Needed
The Gingerbread Golem's Culinary Alchemy: Enchanting Recipes for a Sweetly Dark Feast
A Time Lord Christmas: Holiday Adventures with the Doctor
Krampusproofing Your Home: Defensive Strategies for Yule
Silent Frights: A Collection of Christmas Creepypastas to Chill Your Bones
Santa Raptor's Jolly Carnage: A Dino-Claus Christmas Tale
Prehistoric Palettes: A Dino Wicca Coloring Journey
The Christmas Wishkeeper Chronicles

The Starlight Sleigh: A Holiday Journey
Elf Secrets: The True Magic of the North Pole
Candy Cane Conjurations
Cooking with Kids: Recipes Under 20 Minutes
Doctor Who: The TARDIS Confiscation
The Anxiety First Aid Kit: Quick Tools to Calm Your Mind
Frosty Whispers: A Winter's Tale
The Infinite Key: Unlocking the Secrets to Prosperity, Resilience, and Purpose
The Grasping Void: Why You'll Regret This Purchase
Astrology for Busy Bees: Star Signs Simplified

If you want solar for your home go here: https://www.harborso-lar.live/apophisenterprises/

Get Some Tarot cards: https://www.makeplayingcards.com/sell/apophis-occult-shop

<u>**Get some shirts: https://www.bonfire.com/store/apophis-shirt-emporium/**</u>

<u>**Instagrams:**</u>
@apophis_enterprises,
@apophisbookemporium,
@apophisscardshop
Twitter: @apophisenterpr1
Tiktok:@apophisenterprise
Youtube: @sg1fan23477, @FiresideRetreatKingdom
Hive: @sg1fan23477
CheeLee: @SG1fan23477

Podcast: Apophis Chat Zone: https://open.spotify.com/show/5zXbrCLEV2xzCp8ybrfHsk?si=fb4d4fdbdce44dec

Newsletter: https://apophiss-newsletter-27c897.beehiiv.com/

If you want to support me or see posts of other projects that I have come over to: **buymeacoffee.com/mpetchinskg**
 I post there daily several times a day

Get your Dinowicca or Christmas themed digital products, especially Santa Raptor songs and other musics. Here: **https://sg1fan23477.gumroad.com**

Apophis Yuletide Digital has not only digital Christmas items, but it will have all things with Dinowicca as well as other Digital products.

www.ingramcontent.com/pod-product-compliance
Lightning Source LLC
Chambersburg PA
CBHW070601160726
48003CB00005B/2103